YOUR AUTHOR WEBSITE

WHY YOU NEED ONE AND WHAT IT SHOULD
LOOK LIKE

MARIE WHITE

ZAMIZ PRESS

WRITING/Business Aspects

WRITING/Authorship

ZAMIZ PRESS

Special discounts are available on quantity purchases by corporations, associations and others. For details, contact the author.

DO YOU HAVE A MESSAGE TO SHARE
WITH THE WORLD? ARE YOU INTERESTED IN
HAVING YOUR BOOK PUBLISHED?
VISIT ZAMIZPRESS.COM

Your Author Website: Why You Need One and What it Should Look Like / Marie White — 1st Edition

YOUR FREE GIFT!

What happens when you appear on radio, television, or on a podcast? Find out exactly what to give hosts ahead of time. Grab your copy today at MarieWhiteAuthor.com

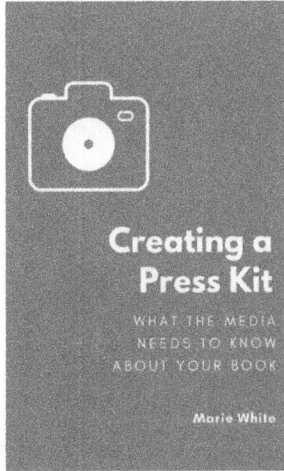

Creating a Press Kit: What the Media Needs to Know About Your Book

CONTENTS

1

FROM INTERESTED TO SOLD

Imagine that you are a guest on your local morning talk show. As you're speaking the host puts a picture of your book on the screen. It is there for four seconds. You mention the name of your book a few times during the interview and then your segment is over.

Someone watching your interview is intrigued. Your book on how to spot the differences between humans and space aliens is exactly what she is looking for. She grabs her phone and types in the name of your book. What was the title again? Oh, wait, it was *Identifying Aliens*. She types the phrase "Edentify Aliens" into the Amazon search bar. Nothing comes up. She gives up and goes on with her day.

You lost the sale because of a misspelled word.

How could this have been avoided?

You could have had a website.

This scenario is even more likely to occur when you have multiple books.

How do you alleviate the pressure of remembering several titles?

You use your name.

Imagine how easy it would be for the viewer to remember that your name is John Smith and that you're an author. In this scenario, she grabs her phone to search the web for "John Smith author." Guess what pops up? Your website www.AuthorJohnSmith.com.

On your website she finds the book she wanted to buy, along with your other books. She clicks on the links to buy your books and then spends a few minutes reading your bio.

She feels like she really knows you.

You've made a connection and she joins your email list.

You will notify her when your next book launches.

The next day she notices that her grandmother's birthday is approaching and returns to your website to order an autographed copy of your latest book.

Grandma will love it.

All this happened because you had a website.

A Turning Point

When my third book came out, I knew that if I wanted people to know about my books, I needed to put myself in the public eye. My first two books hadn't sold well and I didn't want the third one to suffer the same fate.

I saved my pennies and attended every author event, publicity summit, joint venture meeting and local event that I could find.

Meeting people led to more opportunities and more invitations.

Pretty soon I was invited to red carpet events and spoke with people from around the world. I crisscrossed the country promoting my book, from Hollywood to Miami to New York City.

And in every instance, people asked for my website.

I was embarrassed to give them my website address.

While I was in New York City the organizer of TEDx Wilmington, Delaware, invited me to give a TEDx talk and part of the TEDx acceptance process was to look at each speaker's website.

Here were opportunities to promote my third book, but my website was part of the package.

I tinkered with my website, based on what these opportunities required, and each event gave me more insight into the reasons behind having an author website.

If only I'd had a book like this in those beginning years.

Since becoming an author, I have had the privilege of being a guest on more television, radio and podcast shows than I can count. I've flown across the country to give a TEDx talk, created a successful YouTube channel with well over a million views, written eight books and hosted a podcast with coveted celebrity guests. Each of these opportunities has taught me some part of the author website process. Now, I can proudly give out my website address.

But I have to wonder, how many opportunities did I miss because someone visited my website and decided against having me as a guest?

And, why would being a guest on their show matter to an author?

Not Stephen King

When my third book *Strength for Parents of Missing Children* launched, I learned that I needed a website. That wasn't a problem for me, I had created several websites in the past and could easily design one.

But, when I sat down at the computer I was stumped. What in the world should I put on my website?

I searched online for "best author websites." The blogs had some great examples, but they were from successful authors or celebrities, and these websites focused on the person who wrote the book more than on the book itself.

Well, I wasn't Stephen King, so who in the world would care about me?

Based on that assumption, I decided my website couldn't look like a celebrity author site. There would be no big picture of me and no information about what author things I was up to.

I had no events to publicize.

I wasn't going on exotic book tours.

No celebrities were holding my book on Instagram.

Then there were the websites by less famous, yet prolific authors, who had published five, ten, or twenty books. They filled their websites with coming attraction banners, a synopsis of each of their books and a free copy of the first in the series.

I didn't have any of that.

Again, I wondered, "What do I put on my website?"

The first version of my website was basically a white page with three books.

As the year progressed, I attended several events, each of which gave me another piece of the publicity puzzle.

I began to understand how to get publicity and some of the purposes behind my author website.

My website began to evolve.

Now, I'll share those pieces with you.

2

THE PURPOSE OF YOUR WEBSITE

I learned that your website should be the one-stop shop for all your author information. This means that on your site, book-lovers, family, friends, television hosts, show producers, the press, social media followers, and fans should be able to find everything they need to know about you and your books.

A website allows you to deliver your message to the world.

One common misconception is that authors have websites to sell books directly to readers, but most of us don't want to deal with that hassle.

It's that misconception which deters many authors from creating an author website. They simply aren't interested in packing and selling dozens of books through a website. If selling direct isn't your goal, why would you need a website?

. . .

Reasons for a Website

One of the reasons for your website is to give people an idea of who you are and to establish your credibility as an author.

When a local television station wants you to appear on their show, they will visit your website to find out more about you and your books.

- They may also see a book they like and get a copy for themselves.
- The website may help the host come up with questions for the interview.

You can also let people know about upcoming appearances or events where they can meet you.

Your website should:

1. Build your credibility as an author
2. Introduce people to your books
3. Give interviewers a reason to book you
4. Present yourself as a professional
5. Offer signed copies of your books
6. Get people on your email list

Is your website for you? Not really. It's for others, mostly media, to access all the information they need to promote you and your book.

Your author website is also the place where podcast hosts can find out about you, your books and your message. It's a place where fans can connect with you and it establishes your author brand.

A brand consists of the color, theme and message of an author and their books.

If you are the author of three sci-fi books, readers of your first book can go to your website to find your other two books.

Another reason to have a website is to share your accomplishments with those you know and love.

Instead of monopolizing the conversation for hours by describing your writing journey, your book and what you've been up to, sending a link to your author website is a more subtle way of conveying that information.

If you don't feel comfortable emailing your friend to tell them that your book has just won an award, you can include your web address at the bottom of your emails like this:

> *Attached are some pictures of the grandkids. I hope you're having a great summer!*
> *-Marie*
> *MarieWhiteAuthor.com*

If you've included a photo of your award on the website then when they click on the link, they will see your award on the homepage.

3

WHAT'S IN IT FOR ME?

To give an example of WIIFM, imagine that you've written the world's best cat book, it's titled *How to Toilet Train Your Kitten*. You're sure this book will be a huge success because you know that hundreds of thousands of cat owners struggle with the problem of kitten waste daily. Your book is destined to be a bestseller!

As your press release goes out into the world, it ends up on the desks of newspaper editors and radio producers. Unfortunately, your local newspaper editor doesn't have a cat. That means he doesn't know that cat owners are pulling out their hair about this *very* issue. He doesn't know that if he reported on your book, his newspapers would fly off the shelves.

You see, even when someone has written the greatest

book on how to solve a problem, there's no guarantee that it will be publicized.

Your Story

If an editor doesn't see the value in what you have produced, no amount of press release fanfare will entice him to publicize it.

- So, what would prompt an editor to publicize your book?
- What is newsworthy about it?
- What could you say to get your book in front of more people—the people who need your book?

The thing that can get your book in front of people is your story.

Try to find something in the story behind the book or your personal story or a tie-in with current events or a celebrity encounter that gets people's attention. These personal details may make your book noteworthy.

What would interest people enough to listen to you, so that you can end the interview by telling them about your book?

- Have you overcome a hardship or disability?
- Did you move to another country?
- Has your book won an award?

- Are you the head of a club or organization?

Once you find the thing that makes you interesting and learn how to present it, people will want to have you on their shows. They will promote your book while they promote **you.** The audience for your book will find out that your book exists because hosts have promoted **you** on their show.

The people who need to hear about your book will learn about it because **your story** was interesting enough to be featured on the show.

You and your book are a package deal.

When you don't have a website, you reduce your chances of being offered media appearances.

Your website could be the thing that takes your book from obscurity to high visibility.

WIIFM (What's in it for me?)

Your website is the bridge that takes readers from your message to your book. That's a significant reason to have one.

When producers and hosts visit your website, they learn what you have to offer them. That's part of the message you are trying to convey.

You're giving them all the information they need to have you on their program.

When my third book came out, I wanted to write it anonymously. The most important thing to me was to get the information to the people who needed it. *Strength for Parents of Missing Children: Surviving Divorce, Abduction, Runaways and Foster Care* was an inspirational/self-help/non-fiction book. I didn't think that anyone needed to know my personal story.

Being known wasn't important to me.

My message was the important part and I thought I would write it under a pen name so the information would be available to everyone who needed it without my being in the spotlight.

The problem was— no one wanted to carry that story.

Imagine this headline:

> "Unknown Writer Has a Book She
> Wants to Tell You About"

That is *not* a compelling headline. How does that headline help a podcast host, newspaper editor or blogger? It doesn't. There are already books on almost every subject. The media is looking for something newsworthy or interesting to grab their readers' attention. If they don't have it, they won't put it out to the public.

To get their attention you must have an interesting story, an engaging personality, or a cool story-behind-the-story.

Hosts need some reason to have you on their show such as a connection with recent events, a unique angle on a current issue, something unexpected to present or a gimmick that gets people's attention.

When you appear on their show to talk about your

unique angle on a current issue, that's when people will hear about your book and that's when people will start buying it.

The right media coverage can make your book go viral.

This applies to fiction as well.

When you're looking to binge on a book series or escape with a cozy romance, hearing an engaging author speak on the current climate in publishing or how the British monarchy is unlike what is portrayed in "The Crown" is a great introduction to them. If you like their spunky personality, then you might decide to visit their website and while you're there you might grab a book.

How This Works

Imagine that a television producer hears about your world's greatest cat book. The producer asks, "Who is she? What's her website?"

They visit your website looking for:

- Your contact information
- Images of you and your book
- The message you offer their viewers
- Your professionalism
- Awards your book has won
- Reviews
- A link to your book on Amazon, Goodreads or Barnes & Noble

Do you have a website with all the information they need to invite you on their show?

What's in it for me (WIIFM) is the most important question you can answer in interviews and for your readers. The podcast host who visits your website will ask, "WIIFM and my viewers?"

When I thought I could write anonymously I designed a website to present my book.

That website was boring.

Nobody cared about a website about a book.

Let's be honest for a moment.

I don't care about your book.

Why? Because I don't know *you*. I also don't know your book. There are thousands of authors in the world. I don't know why I should care about *you* or *your* book.

Give me a reason to care.

Make me want to know more. It's the same reason we watch the behind-the-scenes footage in movies. We connected with the characters on the screen and now we want to know more.

Make your audience want to know more by connecting with them through your publicity and your website. Invite the audience into your world. If you do that and you're worth knowing, they will follow you to the ends of the earth and you'll have loyal fans.

That's what you're trying to do with your website. You are trying to let the person who is booking guests, the person who is interviewing you, and the person who is setting up the interview, know what's in it for them.

WIIFM is a large part of what authors are answering. That's what the back cover of your book is for. That's what your Amazon description is for. *That* is what your website is for.

4

ELEMENTS OF A GOOD AUTHOR WEBSITE

When I decided to write this book, I asked myself an important question, "Will this book become outdated quickly?" My answer was no, that the key elements of a website would never change.

WIIFM will always be a question people ask. Knowing an author's message, where to find their books and having a way to contact the author, would be timeless elements.

The hardest part for new authors is knowing what to put on the website and understanding exactly what their author website is for.

Imagine you're at a local business event. After the presentation, you stand around talking to people in the room. You end up talking to the host of the local morning radio show. She asks you a few questions and seems interested in having you on the show, but you aren't sure if you answered all her questions correctly.

When she asked, "Is you book available in print?" she meant to ask if it was **only** available in print, since she likes audiobooks and ebooks. When you nodded, your answer was not helpful.

If she visits your website and sees "Get my latest book, available in paperback, ebook and audiobook!" then she has the answer to her question. Why else might she need that answer? What if she's planning an entire show about ebook authors?

This is another example of the value of your author website.

What Not to Include

Don't put everything you are capable of doing on your author website. Research shows that when people have too many options, they feel overwhelmed and don't act. Narrow it down to three things or four of your talents.

Don't try to be all things to all people.

Include These

Key components of a good author website:

- Your author biography (bio)
- Your press kit as a link (optional)

- Your professional author headshot
- Book summary
- Your book's press release
- Book pictures in 3d as well as just the front cover (high resolution)
- Links to your books
- A freebie or option to join your email list (optional)
- A contact form or your email address
- A reason for the reader to visit your website
- Information for media professionals
- A reason for aspiring authors to visit your website (optional)

Now that you realize that your website is not there to boost your ego, it's time to think about all the types of people who will visit it.

- People who want to hire you to teach a class on becoming an author
- An event coordinator who wants to book you as a speaker
- A television host who wants you to come on the show
- The podcaster who wants to book you
- The school administrator who wants you to give a presentation at an assembly
- The blog where you applied to be a quest blogger

These people need to know who you are and what you can do for them. They also want to make sure that you are who you say you are.

When you meet someone, you only know what they tell you. A website with screenshots of your awards, bestseller status and other accolades secure your image as a writing professional.

Some additional things you can include on your website:

- A picture of you at your book table

I don't recommend a picture of yourself at an empty table with one book. Decorate the table. Use the pictures in chapter eight as examples of what engaging author book tables look like. Make your table engaging and specific to your genre. If you write westerns this is a great place to put a horse blanket, a bowl of cowboy figurines, a saddle, or whatever will draw a crowd to your table. Ideally, you would have someone helping you take orders and handle the money. That way you can stand off to the side and talk to people, sign autographs and take pictures.

- A sizzle reel

Think of your website as an interactive business card, resume and movie trailer. For authors who want to have television interviews or speak in front of audiences, a video called a "sizzle reel" gives a 2-4 minute version of your best media or speaking appearances. This allows the media to see if you would be a good fit for the show. They want to know if you will carry yourself well on camera. Will you engage the audience? Will you make the host look good and present your information well? These are a few of the purposes of your sizzle reel. If you don't have any media appearances yet, you could have a friend interview you for 2 minutes and then post that video.

- Your book trailer

Another item that you can include on your website is a trailer for your book. However, I haven't heard of authors making sales because of their book trailers, so this may not be a prudent use of your marketing dollars.

- Links to media interviews

It's important to have a professional author picture taken. Regardless of your financial situation, you should be able to find somewhere to get a headshot done inexpensively. If finances are tight, keep an eye out for coupons.

Why is your picture on the website?

Most media places want to know who they are talking to. They also want to get a feel for who you are. They need to know if you're going to show up wearing an eye patch and a pirate hat. That would be the perfect look for certain programs, but for others.

You want to give the host and producer the best experience possible. If they enjoy you, they may tell other producers about you or recommend you as a guest. If they are disappointed, that will not happen.

What interviewers are looking for:

- Are you professional and do you carry yourself well?
- Do you have things to say and share with their audience?
- Are you an introvert who can't talk on camera?
- Are you afraid to put yourself in the public eye?
- Are you difficult to work with?
- What can you offer their audience? (A free ebook? Advice? Entertaining stories?)
- Is your message inspiring?
- Is your message funny?
- Is your message heartbreaking?
- Is your message seductive?

These are things they need to know ahead of time.

You can answer these questions by having a picture of yourself on the website. That way interviewers will feel like they understand who you are, how you carry yourself and what you look like. If you're a woman named Terry and you mistakenly get booked on a show called *Only Men Today*, a visit to your website will clear up the misunderstanding.

Look at these pre-show advertising images.

Do you see how they used the author photos from my website to create images for their advertising? Each show has its own preferred image format, so they will take your photo and make it work with their image.

Your website should also indicate to them whether you've been on other programs. Is this your first interview? Have you done a thousand interviews and know exactly what to do? Do you have a press kit?

Your press kit would include things like your picture, your book images, a short and long biography, all of your contact information, impressive reader reviews, awards, accomplishments, and sample interview questions.

You've likely seen when authors appear on television programs, that a picture of the book flashes on the screen as the host introduces the author. That's why the show needs a picture of the book. They may also flash your picture on the screen as they talk about you during the show that airs prior to the show you're on.

Your Message

One of the secondary objectives of your author website is to inform hosts, booking agents and producers about your primary message.

If your message is that parenting is a comedy, then you should have that theme on your website. That way the host knows you will tell funny parenting stories when you appear on the show.

If your message is that medical mistakes take lives, then the colors and theme of your site shouldn't be comical. For this type of non-fiction subject, your website might be dark and straight to the point.

The feel and branding of your site should portray your primary message.

This applies to fiction authors as well. You also have a message. Think about what you are offering to your readers. Cozy romance authors offer readers a chance to relax, feel good and have a happy ending. Science-fiction authors offer the intrigue of another world, feeding your imagination with creative characters and unexpected situations.

Take some time to think about what your book offers and what you would like readers, aspiring authors, and the public to know. This becomes your message.

Your message also helps producers know how to use you.

A producer booking you for a show on "How to Become an Author" visits your website and sees that your message is that parenting is comedy. The producer may realize that you would be the perfect guest for the morning show episode on parenting. If this happens, you could talk about your book on both shows.

Your website is your virtual calling card.

It's your virtual press kit.

It's all the information a producer or host needs to know.

Style

The look or style of your website will change. The format that was popular for author websites ten years ago is not the same as the format that is popular today. Today, we optimize author websites for mobile viewing. That means your website needs to look great on a desktop, laptop, tablet, and smartphone. Three years from now they may change again, but the core information included on your website will remain the same. People will always need to know your message, how to reach you, what you write, where your books are available and who you are.

A great author website can raise you above the crowd.

For design inspiration, let's look at the websites of famous authors and see how their teams build a website.

5

EVALUATING FAMOUS AUTHOR WEBSITES

When you want website ideas, visit some of the bestselling authors in your genre. Take a look at world-famous author John Grisham's website.

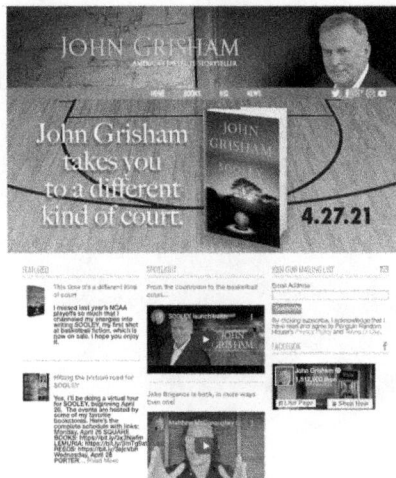

Starting from the top of the page we can see the author's name, what he's known for and what he looks like. In the center we see a 3D version of his latest book, the date it became available and a little about the book. Below that we see three columns, starting with written publicity that his new books have received. The second column has a video trailer and a celebrity endorsement. The third column contains a call to action to join his mailing list, as well as a link to his main social media page.

What is the feel of this website? Would anyone accidentally conclude that he was a writer of light comedy or cozy romance?

Notice the colors that have been chosen to represent this author. The author has a serious look on his face. The background of his headshot is black and the banner across the top is in gray tones. These are strategic decisions, made to convey that the author writes about serious subjects. His tagline "American's Favorite Storyteller," tells you what you need to know about him.

You don't need a tagline on your website, but if you had one, what would yours say?

This is the website of bestselling Christian author Francine Rivers.

Starting from the top, we see a call to action to subscribe to her newsletter. Across from that, we see a link to the movie made from one of her books. Below that we see a banner with her name and clickable tabs that take you to specific pages within her website. The tabs are home, about, books, blog, life with Francine, media, contact and her social media links. Finally, we see Francine's author headshot and her title "Internationally Bestselling Author."

Francine's website is quite long. The rest of her homepage has not been included, but it contains clickable images of each of her books and summaries to the right of them.

What feel does this homepage convey? Does it feel as serious as John Grisham's? Do you think she writes sci-fi or comedy? Does she give the impression that she is a well-known author?

For our last evaluation, let's look at George R. R. Martin's homepage.

At first glance, what type of books do you think George writes? Is there any chance that a new visitor would mistake George for a self-help author? Notice the color choices and medieval design elements on the page.

I'll point out some of the unique features of this webpage.

1. There is no author headshot (every rule is made to be broken, especially by celebrities)
2. He named his blog "Not a Blog"
3. He has a page just for fans
4. He has a storefront for branded merchandise
5. He has a block with his upcoming appearances
6. He has a block for next publications, even though his fans have been waiting years for this last book

George also has all the essential elements that we discussed in previous chapters.

For an example of a non-fiction author website, visit MarieWhiteAuthor.com.

Visit heathbrothers.com to see an outstanding example of a co-author website.

Go to the websites of three or four famous authors in your genre to get some inspiration for your own site. Consider the elements you like from each site.

Thoughts you'll want to write down:

- I like this banner
- I like that font
- The color scheme matches my covers
- I could make my own version of this advertisement

Things You Can't Do

There are some things you won't be able to do. Most people won't be able to write "NYT Bestselling Author" on their website. If you're a first-time author and most authors in your genre have links to their previously published books, you won't have that. You may also be missing a blog, interview photos and celebrity endorsements. I'm also guessing that you don't have a Nobel Peace Prize. No problem. Work with what you have. Do you have a 5-star review, a writing award or a photo of you and a celebrity? Use those to build credibility.

In the beginning your credibility builder may be a review from your mother. "'I couldn't put this book down!' -Ma Smith."

As the number and quality of your reviews grow, you can remove these early quotes and insert more influential ones.

Look through popular author websites, then emulate what you can and write down other ideas for future updates to your site.

Now that we've spent some time going over what a great author website looks like, it's time to work on yours!

6

WEBSITE ADDRESS AND HOSTING

In previous chapters, we discussed the easiest way to turn a casual listener or viewer into a customer.

Imagine how easy it would be for the viewer to remember that your name is John Smith and that you're an author. In this scenario, she grabs her phone to search the web for "John Smith author." Guess what pops up, www.AuthorJohnSmith.com.

On your website she finds the book she wanted to buy, along with your other books. She clicks on the links to buy your books and then spends a few minutes reading your bio. She feels like she really knows you. You've made a connection through your bio and she joins your email list, so she is notified when your next book launches.

The next day she notices that her grandmother's birthday is coming up and returns to your website to order an autographed copy of your latest book. Grandma will love it.

All this happened because you had a website.

Your URL

You'll notice that the website address, called a URL, is the author's name plus the word "author" and dot com. This is a great way for your website to appear at the top of searches on search engines such as DuckDuckGo and Google.

I recommend this as the best way to format your website address, either Yournameauthor.com or Authoryourname.com.

If your name is taken, here are some variations:

Yournamewriter.com

Writeryourname.com

Yournameauthorofgenre.com

(JaneDoeAuthorofFantasy.com)

Authorofgenreyourname.com

(AuthorofFantasyJaneDoe.com)

.   .   .

I do not recommend using alternate ending URLs such as:

.us

.net

.co

Most people think of URLs as ending with ".com". That means the first time they type in your name they are going to go to the wrong website. When you want to find something online in a hurry, how long will you spend writing and rewriting URLs until you find the right one?

Authors who use these alternate URL endings often do so because they have a vision in mind that includes a particular name for their website. However, your potential readers don't care about your vision. They care about finding you with ease. They care about satisfying their desire to escape into a fantasy or learn something through your books. They have no interest in the vision for your website.

Don't make finding you more difficult than necessary.

People like things to be easy. When you make things hard, you lose their interest and goodwill.

You are trying to woo the reader, not turn them off.

To purchase your custom domain name (URL) you can type "purchase domain name" in your search bar or go to a domain name service such as godaddy.com.

If you have absolutely no money to spend on your dream of becoming an author, having a custom URL is not a necessity. Many of the websites that pop up when you type "free website" into your browser offer a free website with their name on it, such as Authormichaelblack.yolasite.com.

Don't allow money to stop you. Get the free URL and keep moving forward.

Web Hosting

There are many free web hosting websites to choose from. Some of the ones I have used and can recommend are Yola.com, Wix.com and Wordpress.com.

These websites are free and easy to use. They do not require any technical knowledge. They operate very much like a Word document, with templates and buttons to click, as well as added features. Each of them have tutorials available on their website. In addition you can visit YouTube and search "Wix website tutorial." YouTube also contains specific parts you may need help with, such as "how to add a video to a Yola website."

These websites will give you the option of purchasing your custom URL through them. Often the first year is at a very reduced price.

Once you have chosen your free website host, it's time to begin laying out your website.

Layout

In writing, there are planners and then there are those who fly by the seat of their pants. It is the same in website design. Some people design their website on paper before looking for a similar template, while others find a template they love and make it work. The choice is yours.

I recommend sketching your layout ahead of time, based on the websites you looked at and the elements we covered in chapters three and four.

Join me in the next chapter to begin the sketching process.

7

BUILDING YOUR WEBSITE

In the beginning, most new authors can get away with a simple, one-page website. This is the easiest and most economical to build. Once you have hundreds of views on your page and additional information to incorporate, you can add more pages.

If you already have a website, update it every 18-24 months. Use this chapter to give your website an update with any of the elements you feel are beneficial.

Your goal is also to present yourself as a professional author, regardless of your full or part-time writer status.

Begin by sketching what you think your author website should look like based on the websites we looked at in chapter five. I recommend using a pencil, as you will probably make several changes along the way.

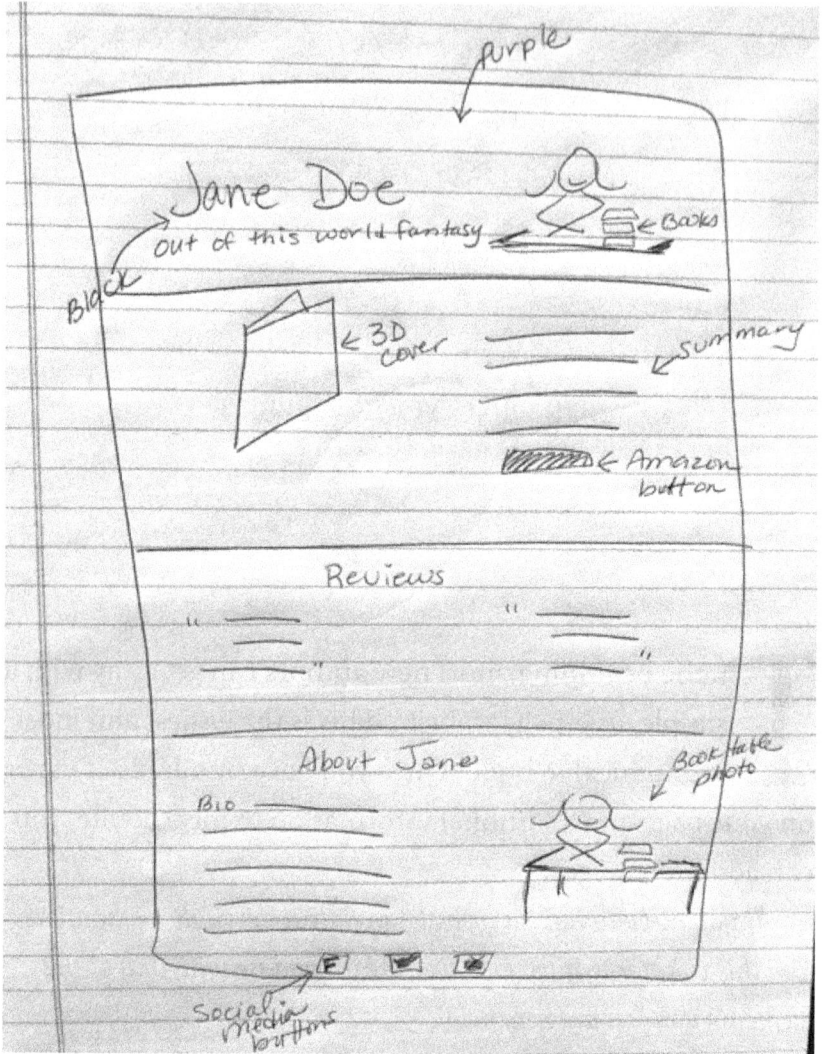

Brand

What color immediately comes to mind when you think of Coca Cola®?

What color comes to mind when you think of Starbucks®?

These companies have a color and brand image that matches what they sell. If you sell cozy romance or children's picture books, then a black website with red lettering may not match what you sell. If you sell business books, what colors would convey the message of authority, competence, and leadership? Is your book political? If so, the tie you wear in your headshot might be the color of your political party and you could use that color used throughout your website, book covers and marketing materials.

Having a personal brand color makes creating fliers, bookmarks, business cards, and your website much simpler. You already have a starting point, your color. Look at your book cover.

Is there a color on the cover that stands out to you?

What color do you look best in?

Once you find your signature color, it becomes easier to find pictures for the website, as they must compliment your brand's color scheme. Designing your branded goodies for book signings, speaking events, and book tables is simple when you have a signature color.

A brand message helps you present yourself as an authority on that subject. It also helps you cut out things that don't fit your brand image. If you're a children's book author, you probably wouldn't put pictures of yourself attending an erotica convention. Why? Because erotica and children's picture books are not compatible as a brand.

I don't display a message on my website, but I know what my brand message is.

I am the director of publishing for Zamiz Press and our brand message is "Publishing with Integrity." Every word that we write on the website should fit within that message. If we wanted to vent about an issue, we wouldn't do it. Why? Because it wouldn't fit our brand message. Negative comments about other companies would not be compatible with the goal of serving our clients with integrity.

It's the same with your author brand. If you write books on business strategy, then putting a collection of Bigfoot drawings on your website would contradict your brand. The drawings wouldn't go on the website.

Your Book Picture

Do you have an excellent picture of your book? If so, place it on your website and include links to your book on the major booksellers such as Amazon and Barnes & Noble. Describe your book so that visitors understand what your book is about.

Your Other Pages

Have you created your Amazon Author Central page? Do

you have an author page on Goodreads? Put a link to any author pages you have.

Media

Add pictures and links to your media appearances, guest blog posts, videos about you and reviews of your book.

Bio or About the Author

Invite readers and media into your story so they can cheer you on.

Wins

Put your wins on the website. Has your book won an award or received a coveted endorsement? Has a celebrity noticed your book? These wins will help you build your reputation and credibility.

Recent Happenings

Show your most recent blog post or guest blog post. Have you published an article or been featured on a show?

Pictures

When I am a podcast guest, hosts generally ask me for a

picture, my bio and an image of my latest book. Because all of that is all available on my website, they often get the information they need without having to ask me for it. When I appear on the show, I notice that they took the pictures they needed directly from my website.

Options

Sometimes show producers need a picture of the front cover of your book and sometimes they want a 3D version of your cover. Most of the time they make the 3D version themselves, so they will ask for the front cover only.

If you have created an ad for Facebook or other social media apps, you can include a picture of the ad on your website as well. Shows may put your ad on the screen while you're speaking or ahead of your interview.

"Tune in tomorrow when we have author Jane Doe on the show, talking about how you can become an author."

As he speaks these words, your advertisement, or book, or picture flashes across the screen.

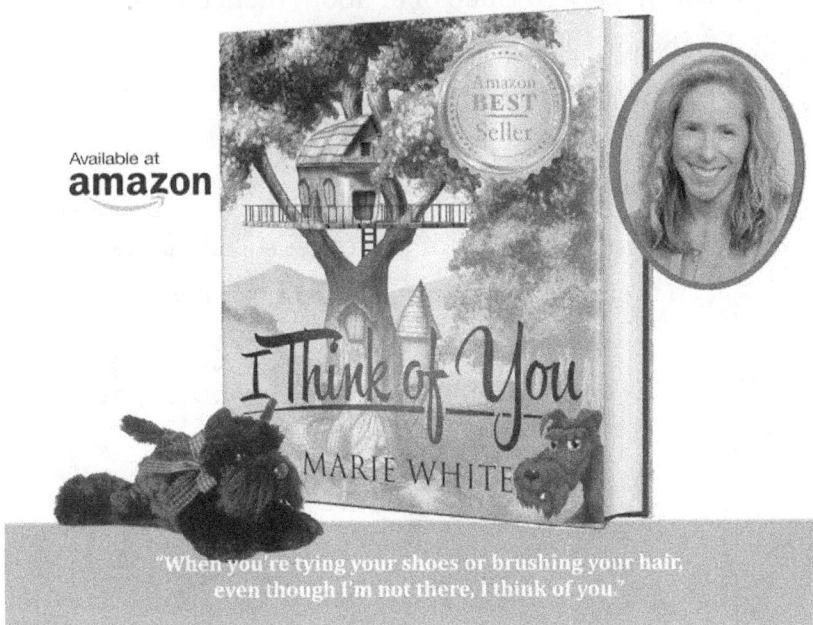

Homework

Watch an interview on YouTube of one of your favorite authors or of a famous author. While you're watching the interview, pay attention to whether their website is mentioned. Pause the interview and visit their website.

Think about these things:

- What did you go to their website to find?
- Did they have any upcoming events?
- Did they have any new books coming out or recently released?
- Have they won any awards?
- Did you find a video of or about them on the website?
- Has he/she written anything you didn't know about?
- How did he/she get started?
- Is he/she on Twitter or any other social media?
- Did their website answer these questions?

These are the same questions people who visit your site will ask.

8

THE FINAL PIECE

When you are invited to appear on podcasts, television shows and radio programs, make sure you provide the show with your website URL at least one day before your interview. At the end of your interview, remember to mention that "viewers can find me at www.--------.com."

Just as we talked about the brand, colors, message and layout of your website, it's also important to talk about your author book table.

Most authors have dreamed of presenting their books to the world. Having a book signing or taking part in an outdoor book display may be part of that dream.

I attended the two largest books fairs in the United States, the Miami Book Fair and the Los Angeles Times Festival of the Book. At both, I saw authors who simply brought along their books, as well as authors who came prepared with a full book display.

When I wasn't at my book table, I wandered the fair and talked with other authors. I made a point to stop at the tables of authors who sat alone, in the sun, with an empty table and a stack of books. It broke my heart.

Authors can create an engaging book table with very little money. Wire display stands and a black or gold tablecloth from your local dollar store will give your book the perfect backdrop.

Add a bowl of candy, a clipboard with paper to collect email addresses, and a few decorative items that match your theme, and your table will look presentable!

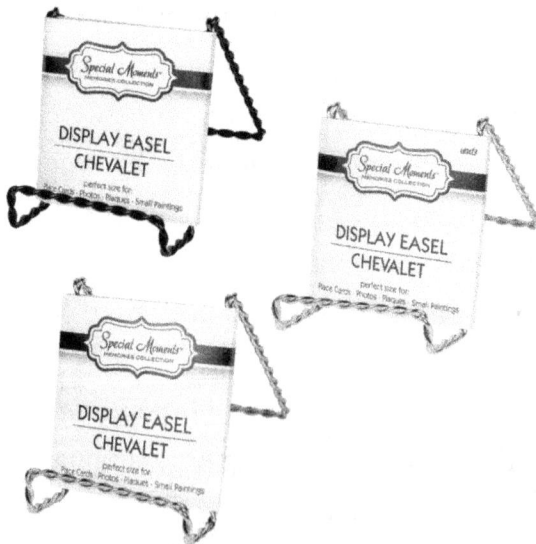

Authors with a larger budget can purchase a black cloth

tablecloth, customized table runner, branded giveaways (key chains, bookmarks, stickers, or pens,) and coordinating toys.

Children's book authors can look at giveaways including similarly themed erasers, baskets of plush toys and large display stuffed animals. They can also consider wearing a costume or running a contest.

Excellent author book table examples:

Wrap it Up

Writers are artists. This book has been a simple guide to get your creative juices flowing while you design your website. I hope you've been inspired as you evaluated successful author websites and learned the key elements of a great homepage.

Your quest for the perfect website will never end. Every time I look at mine, I see an area that I should update or improve. Like our books, at some point we must leave well-enough alone.

The beauty of designing your own website is that you have complete creative control. If you wake up in the middle of the night with a creative idea, you can hop out of bed and implement it!

We've discussed the key elements of a great website and looked at successful author websites. I've given you tools to scrutinize other author websites so that you can find the best elements for your site. You've answered tough questions about your brand message and sketched out your new author homepage.

For first-time authors, creating an author website can seem confusing and intimidating, but it doesn't have to be. With the tools in this book you can make your website stand out from the crowd. I'll be on the sidelines, cheering you on.

If you haven't already started your website, today is a great day to start!

Once you finish, send me the link at MarieWhiteAuthor.com!

ABOUT THE AUTHOR

Marie White is the author of eight books, including the multiple award-winning #1 bestseller *Strength for Parents of Missing Children: Surviving Divorce, Abduction, Runaways and Foster Care*. She is a TEDx speaker and the director of publishing at Zamiz Press. You can find her videos as the host of "Bible Stories for Adults" on YouTube, with well over a million views. She encourages people from all walks of life and experiencing a variety of struggles, to know that there is hope.

Readers can connect with Marie at MarieWhiteAuthor.com.

Her books include the children's books, *Sophia Wants to Write a Book* and *I Think of You,* as well as the adult books, *Changing Your Life in Just Ten Days, Ten Day Bible Study*, and many more.

Hello, Marie!

Books

Marie White is the author of eight books, including the multiple award-winning #1 bestseller "Strength for Parents of Missing Children: Surviving Divorce, Abduction, Runaways and Foster Care". She is also a TEDx speaker, traveler, entrepreneur and the host of "Bible Stories for Adults" on YouTube with over a million views. She encourages people from all walks of life and experiencing a variety of struggles, to know that there is hope.

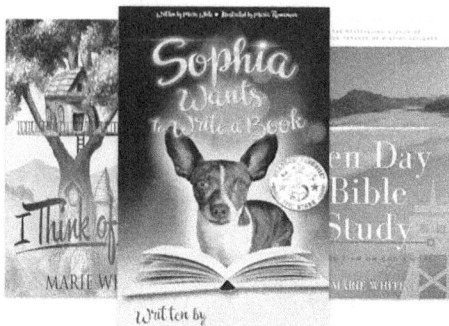

More Books by Marie

If you've enjoyed this book, check out these additional titles by Marie White.

Available at
amazon

"When you're tying your shoes or brushing your hair, even though I'm not there, I think of you."

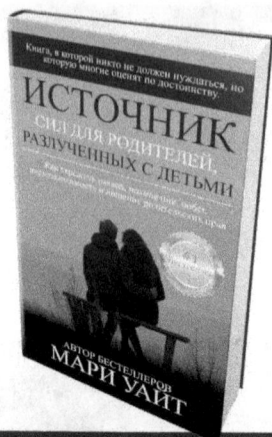

Вы не одиноки.

Мари взяла боль своей семьи и превратила ее в путеводитель, которого не было у нее.

И теперь я чувствую надежду!

www.ingramcontent.com/pod-product-compliance
Lightning Source LLC
Chambersburg PA
CBHW060258030426
42335CB00014B/1755